Buzz and Bingo
in the
Starry Sky

Written by Alan Durant
Illustrated by Sholto Walker

Collins

Chapter 1

One starry night, Buzz was looking at the sky through a telescope.

"I can see the Great Bear," he said to Bingo. "Look, there's Little Bear, too. There's Orion the hunter, with his glittering belt. Oh, and there's a star for you, Bingo – the dog star, Sirius. It's very bright. Come and see."

Bingo jumped up on to a stool and looked through the telescope at Sirius.

"Woof!" he barked, wagging his tail.

Buzz saw something flash across the sky. "That must be a shooting star, Bingo," he said. "I wonder where it's going."

WUMP!

Something thumped to the ground outside and made the house shake. Buzz jumped and Bingo fell off the stool.

"Whatever can that be?" said Buzz. "I don't think shooting stars land on Earth."

Buzz opened the front door and went outside.

"Look, Bingo!" he cried. A small spaceship had landed in the front garden. A door beeped open and a little green face peered out.

"Greetings, people," said a squeaky, shaky voice. "Can you tell me, please, what planet I am on?"

"Greetings," said Buzz. "I'm Buzz and this is my dog Bingo. You're on planet Earth."

"Woof!" said Bingo.

The little alien started to cry. "My name's XY5," he sniffed, "and I want my mummy."

Buzz took the little alien inside. He gave him a biscuit and a beaker of orange juice. XY5 swallowed the biscuit in one bite and drank the juice in one gulp. Then he ate the beaker, too!

"Yum, yum," he sighed. "You have delicious food on your planet."

"Yes," said Buzz with a frown. "Now, tell us where you come from."

The alien started to look sad again. "I come from the planet ICU."

"Where's that?" Buzz asked.

"Next to the planet ICU2," said XY5. "Do you know it?"

Buzz shook his head.

"Oh," said the alien sadly.

Buzz gave him another biscuit and another beaker of orange juice.

"How did you come to land on Earth?" he asked.

"Yesterday was my birthday, and my mum and dad gave me a new spaceship," said XY5. "I was taking it for a ride when a meteor storm blew up and I couldn't see where I was going. Now I'm completely lost. I'll never see my home or my family again." Green tears trickled down the little alien's face.

"Don't cry," said Buzz. "Bingo and I will help you get home again. We love adventures, don't we, Bingo?"

Bingo said nothing. He was busy licking up the biscuit crumbs.

Chapter 2

Buzz, Bingo and XY5 got on board the little alien's spaceship.

"Hold on tight!" said XY5. He flicked a switch, turned a dial, pulled a lever and … whoosh! The small spaceship flew up into the sky.

"Wow!" said Buzz as he looked out of the window at the starry sky. "This is amazing, isn't it, Bingo?"

Bingo just whimpered. He was feeling spacesick!

"The problem is, I don't know which way to go," said XY5, "and there aren't any signposts in space."

"Look, there's Great Bear," said Buzz. "Let's ask him."

Great Bear had never heard of the planet ICU. He had a problem of his own.

"I've lost Little Bear," he said. "Have you seen him?"

"No," said Buzz. "But if we do, I'll tell him you're looking for him."

"Thanks," said Great Bear.

XY5 pulled the lever and the spaceship flew on.

They hadn't gone far when they met Orion, the hunter. But he didn't know the way to ICU either.

"I've lost my belt," he said. "Have you seen it?"

"No," said Buzz. "But we'll look out for it on our way."

Then off they flew once more.

They met Draco the dragon,

the twins Castor and Pollux,

the seven sisters

and Pegasus the winged horse,
galloping across the Milky Way.

But none of them knew
the way to the planet ICU.

Suddenly, Bingo started to bark.

"There's Sirius, the dog star," said Buzz. "He's snarling.
I wonder why?"

"Perhaps he's lost his way, too," said XY5.

But Sirius hadn't lost his way – he'd lost his bone!

"We'd better look for that, too," said Buzz.

"Woof," barked Bingo happily. He loved looking for bones!

Chapter 3

The space ship flew on until it came to the planet Mars. There were little green men there, but they weren't very friendly, so the travellers quickly moved on.

They passed by Jupiter and then wove through the rings of Saturn. But still there was no sign of ICU.

"I'll never get home," sobbed XY5.

Whoosh, whirr! Suddenly the spaceship started to spin.

"What's happening?" yelled Buzz.

"I don't know," cried XY5. "The controls aren't working. Something's got hold of us."

The spaceship hurtled upwards.

"Woof, woof!" barked Bingo, as he rolled this way and that.

Round and round spun the spaceship until at last ...

... clang! It landed somewhere very dark.

"I wonder where we are?" said Buzz.

"I don't know," said XY5. "But I don't like it."

Bingo barked very quietly. He didn't like it either.

Then lights went on outside the spaceship. A large green face peered in through the window.

"Mummy!" yelled XY5. He turned to Buzz with a huge smile. "I'm home," he said happily.

XY5 introduced Buzz to his family.

"This is my mum, Y and this is my dad, X," he said. "These are my brothers and sisters, XY1, XY2, XY3, XY4 and the baby, XY6."

"Pleased to meet you all," said Buzz. "My name's Buzz and this is my dog, Bingo."

"Woof!" barked Bingo and he wagged his tail.

"We come from the planet Earth," said Buzz.

"Thank you so much for bringing our son home," said X.

"It was a pleasure," said Buzz, "But I'm not quite sure how we got here."

"Ah, I'll show you," said X. He took Buzz and Bingo
to a viewing station. There, below them, was an enormous
machine that looked just like a giant vacuum cleaner.

"I thought XY5 might be lost, so I turned on the Max Attract,"
said X. "It pulls in anything from light years around."

"Mmm, I see," said Buzz. He stared hard at the Max Attract
for a moment or two. Suddenly he had an idea.

"Could I take a look inside your machine?" he asked.

"Of course," replied X.

Buzz, XY5 and X climbed down into the Max Attract.
As Buzz had suspected, XY5's spaceship wasn't
the only thing caught there. Inside the machine Buzz found
a glittering belt, an enormous bone and ... Little Bear!

"Oh dear," said XY5's dad. "I don't know where these things came from."

"I do," laughed Buzz. "Bingo and I will take them back to where they belong on our way home."

"Thank you," said XY5's dad. "XY5 and I will give you a lift in our family spaceship."

"It's a *people* carrier," said XY5 proudly.

Buzz and Bingo said goodbye to XY5's mum and his brothers
and sisters. Then they blasted off from the planet ICU with
XY5 and his dad, back into space.

On the way home they took Little Bear to Great Bear.

They gave Orion his belt …   … and Sirius his bone.

At last the spaceship arrived at Buzz and Bingo's house.

"Goodbye," said Buzz. "Drop by anytime."

"Maybe when I'm a bit older," said XY5. "I wouldn't want to get lost again."

"Bingo and I would love another space adventure," said Buzz, "wouldn't we, Bingo?"

But Bingo was already inside the house. He was back on Earth and that's where he was going to stay.

🐾 Ideas for reading 🐾

Written by Linda Pagett B.Ed (hons), M.Ed
Lecturer and Educational Consultant

Reading objectives:
- predict what might happen on the basis of what has been read so far
- discuss and clarify the meanings of words
- make inferences on the basis of what is being said and done
- check that the text makes sense to them as they read and correcting inaccurate reading

Spoken language objectives:
- use spoken language to develop understanding through speculating, imagining and exploring ideas
- give well-structured descriptions, explanations and narratives for different purposes, including for expressing feelings
- maintain attention and participate actively in collaborative conversations
- participate in discussions and role play

Curriculum links: Citizenship

Interest words: telescope, Sirius, shooting star, alien, Castor, Draco, Great Bear, ICU, Jupiter, Little Bear, Max Attract, meteor, Orion, Pegasus, people carrier, Pollux, Saturn, spacesick

Word count: 1,267

Resources: whiteboard

Build a context for reading

This book can be read over two or more reading sessions.

- Introduce the book by its cover. Ask the children what they can predict about Buzz and Bingo from the cover and the title page. Some may recognise the characters from Collins Big Cat books *Buzz and Bingo in the Fairytale Forest* and *Buzz and Bingo in the Monster Maze.*

- Ask the children to predict what the book is about. *Where is the story set and what might the characters be like? What else might you find in space?*

- Discuss with the children what they know about space. *What is found there (stars, planets, moons)? How big do you think space is?*

- Show the children the chart of the night sky on pp30-31and ask them to find the different star groups, also known as constellations: *Big Bear, Little Bear, Pegasus* and *Orion.* Explain that the names were given because astronomers thought the pattern of the stars were like the shapes of animals or heroes (model this on a whiteboard if necessary).

Understand and apply reading strategies

- Ask the children to read silently up to p9 and then ask them about the story so far. How is the young alien feeling? What can Buzz and Bingo do to help (or what would the children do to help)? What will happen next?

- Ask them to read on independently quietly up to page 29. Listen to each child read a short passage aloud, prompting and praising their use of strategies for solving unfamiliar words.

The night sky

Little Bear

Seven Sisters

Great Bear

Sirius

Pegasus

Twins

Orion

Draco